ADVENTURES WITH A CARDBOARD TUBE

ADVENTURES WITH A

CARDBOARD TUBE

FIRST SCIENCE EXPERIMENTS

by HARRY MILGROM

illustrated by TOM FUNK

E. P. DUTTON & CO., INC. NEW YORK

Published simultaneously in Canada by Clarke,
Irwin & Company Limited, Toronto and Vancouver

SBN: 0–525–25150–2   LCC: 71–179045

Printed in the U.S.A.
First Edition

To my grandson Marc Damon Milgrom
and all the other grandchildren who
will help shape the future of mankind

A cardboard tube is a handy object for exploring science.

Collect some cardboard tubes at home. Aluminum foil, paper towels, plastic wrap, and waxed paper are rolled on cardboard tubes.

6.

Ask your mother to save the empty tubes for you.   7.

What is the shape of your tube?

It is a circle on end.

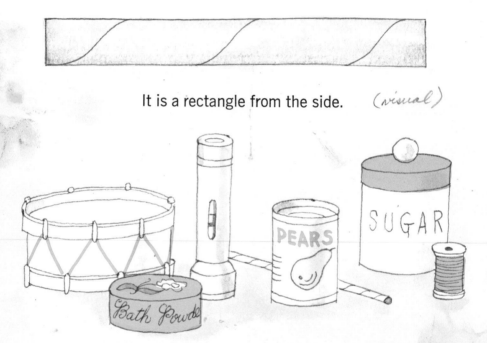

It is a rectangle from the side. *(visual)*

An object with such a shape is called a cylinder.

A cardboard tube is a cylinder.

How many different kinds of cylinders can you find in your house?

8.   Look around.

Place a tube on the floor.

Give the tube a push.

What happens?

The tube rolls along in a straight line.

The cardboard tube is a roller.

9.

What happens to the circle when you squeeze one end of the tube?

The circle becomes an oval.

What becomes of the oval when you let go of the tube?

The oval springs back into a circle.

The cardboard tube is like a spring.

Squash one end of a tube.

How will this tube roll on the floor?

Will it roll in a straight line or will it roll in some other path?

Try it.

The tube with the squashed end rolls in a straight line!

The distance around both ends remains the same even though one is squashed.

The tube continues to roll in a straight line.   11.

Tape

Color one end of a tube black.

visual?

Hold the tube one foot above a table.

What happens when you let go?

The tube falls, hits the table, and bounces.

Hold the tube three feet above the table.

Let go.

What happens now?

The tube bounces and the black end flips over from one side to the other.

12.

Drop the tube from higher and higher positions.

Does the tube flip over twice? three times?

What is the most times you can get the tube to flip over?

Does your tube ever flip over and remain standing on one end?

Try to get your tube to do this.

How often does the tube land on its end?

Make a hill with a piece of
stiff cardboard on two books.

Let a tube roll down from the top of the hill.

How many inches does it roll before it comes to a stop?

Fill the tube with pencils and pens to make it heavier.

Let it roll down again.

How many inches does the tube roll this time before
it comes to a stop?

What does this show?

14.   A weighted tube rolls farther than an empty one.

Place a book on the table.

Blow against the book.

What happens?

Place the same book on two tubes.

Blow against the book.

What happens now?

15.

Can a cardboard tube hold up more weight
on its side or on its end without caving in?

Pile books on the tube in each position.

The tube on its end can hold up more weight
without caving in than the tube on its side.

16.

Look through a tube at the words on this page.

You see the words clearly.

Touch the page with the tube.

What do you see when the tube touches the page?

When the tube touches the page, no light reaches the words. Without light you cannot see the words.

visual

With a cardboard tube you can put a make-believe hole in your hand.

Hold the palm of your right hand in front of your right eye.

Place the tube against the side of your right hand as shown.

Look through the tube with your left eye.

When you look with both eyes, your right hand will seem to have a hole in its palm.

Your left eye sees the hole in the tube.

Your right eye sees your hand.

Your brain blends the two separate views.

You think you see a hole in your hand.

Hold one end of a tube against your right ear.

What do you hear?

Hold a second tube against your left ear.

What do you hear?

All the sounds around you go into the tubes.

There the sounds come together to produce one big sound that you hear as a roar.

18.

Take two tubes of the same size.

Cut one in half.

Tap one end of the long tube against a table.

At the same time tap one end of the short tube also.

What do you notice?

Both tubes vibrate and give off sounds.

20. The short tube makes a higher sound than the long tube.

Blow across the short tube.

Blow across the long tube.

What do you notice?

Blowing air across the top of a tube produces a sound.

In this case also the short tube gives off a higher
sound than the long tube.

21.

Stand a tube on a table.

Blow against the tube, not across it.

What happens?

The air pushes against the tube and overturns it.

22.   Moving air can make things move.

Fill one end of a tube with an inch or two of modeling clay (plasticine).

Stand the weighted end of this tube on the table.

Blow against the tube.

What happens now?

It is harder to overturn the weighted tube.

23.

Adding weight to the bottom of an object helps prevent its overturning.

24.   Cars are weighted at the bottom for this reason.

Place the weighted end of the tube on the edge of the table.

Let the unweighted part stick out past the edge.

Why doesn't the tube fall off the table?

When the short, weighted part of the tube balances the long, unweighted part, the tube remains balanced on the edge of the table without falling off.

How can a tube be used for comparing weights of different objects?

Make a balance scale.

Cut off the hook of a wire clothes hanger with wire-cutting pliers.

Bend the rest of the wire to form a stand.

With scissors cut the ends of a cardboard tube to form the pans of the scale.

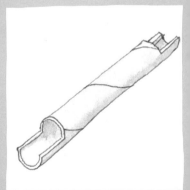

With a pencil poke a hole in the upper middle part of the tube.

Slide a two-inch piece of plastic or paper straw through this hole.

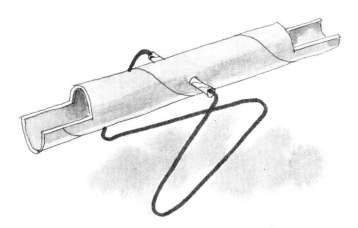

Place the ends of the wire stand into the straw to complete the scale, as shown.

Put a penny on one side of the scale and paper clips on the other side.

Find out how many paper clips it takes to balance a penny.

Do the same thing with a nickel and a quarter.

Think of other objects to compare.

Use your homemade scale to weigh all the things that come to your mind.

28.

Now you know what a cardboard tube is and that it does many wonderful things.

A cardboard tube is a CYLINDER.

A cardboard tube rolls in a STRAIGHT LINE.

A cardboard tube is like a SPRING.

A cardboard tube can bounce and flip over.

A heavy tube rolls farther than a light one.

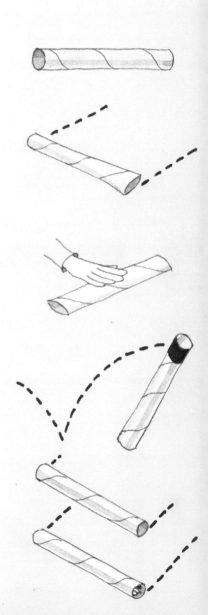

A cardboard tube is a WEIGHT-MOVER.

A cardboard tube is a LIGHT-BLOCKER.

A cardboard tube is a SOUND-COLLECTOR.

A cardboard tube is a SOUND-MAKER.

A cardboard tube is a BALANCE SCALE.

What else can you find out about a cardboard tube?

Think of what you want to do.

Try it.

See what you can discover.   31.

HARRY MILGROM is Director of Science of the New York City Public Schools. He has devised many new materials and techniques for teaching science. He is also founding director of Science I, a Saturday program for children that he conducts at the Dalton School in Manhattan. Mr. Milgrom is also the author of *First Experiments with Gravity* and the *Adventures* series.

TOM FUNK illustrated *Adventures with a String* by Harry Milgrom. He has done the drawing for a number of other children's books, including *The Terrible Terrier*. He has also done freelance illustration for magazines and greeting cards. Mr. Funk lives with his family in Westport, Connecticut.